GEORGE BUSH

THE STORY OF

The Forty-first President of the United States

BY MARK SUFRIN

A YEARLING BOOK

About This Book

The events described in this book are true. They have been carefully researched and excerpted from authentic autobiographies, writings, and commentaries. No part of this biography has been fictionalized.

To learn more about George Bush, ask your librarian to recommend other fine books you might read.

Published by
Dell Publishing
a division of
Bantam Doubleday Dell Publishing Group, Inc.
666 Fifth Avenue
New York, New York 10103

ISBN: 0-440-40174-7

Published by arrangement with Parachute Press, Inc.

Printed in the United States of America
February 1989

10 9 8 7 6 5 4 3 2 1

Contents

"Have-half" Bush

George Herbert Walker Bush was born on June 12, 1924, in Milton, Massachusetts. He was the second oldest of five children, four boys and a girl. When he was a small boy, the family moved to Greenwich, Connecticut. Greenwich was a beautiful town with big comfortable houses. It had fine schools and lots of open space where children could play. Many businessmen who worked in New York City lived there. George's father, Prescott Bush, a banker, traveled to New York City every day.

Prescott and Dorothy Bush were a great influence on their children. Mr. Bush, who became a U.S. senator, taught his sons duty and service. George Bush credits his mother with giving him his great ability to get along with people. Both of George's parents were good athletes and taught their children to love sports. Mr. Bush often took George and his older brother, Prescott, Jr., to Yankee Stadium in New York City. George enjoyed these outings and dreamed of playing first base someday. Mrs. Bush was a small woman, but she was a fine golfer and tennis player. She also played basketball and baseball with her children, and, according to George, won every foot race. Even when her teenage sons outgrew her, she could still compete with them.

The Bushes didn't spoil their children. They corrected and punished them when necessary. But it was always for their own good.

"They were our biggest boosters," said Bush, "always there when we needed them. It taught me to be the same way with my own children."

Religious teaching was also part of the Bush home. Every morning at breakfast George's mother or father read the children a Bible lesson. The family was Episcopalian and attended Christ Church in Greenwich.

Prescott Bush raised his children to work hard to earn money for the things they wanted. If young George or his brothers or sister wanted a new baseball glove or skates, they did odd jobs around town to earn money. They mowed lawns, cleaned garages, shoveled snow, ran errands—anything that would pay. From an early age they were taught an important lesson. If an illness or something serious happened, their parents would be there to help. But once they left home, they would have to make it on their own. Prescott Bush also felt that the more advantages a person had, the more public service he or she should offer. After Prescott Bush made his mark in the business world, he served two terms as United States senator from Connecticut.

George Bush grew into a tall, slim, handsome teenager. He was a fine athlete and popular with both boys and girls. But what people remember most about him was how unselfish he was. His family nickname was George "Have-half" Bush. His mother, in her late eighties, said he was always taking friends or stray kids he picked up into the family kitchen, offering food. "Here, have half," he would say.

The Bushes were a close, happy family,

but never as close or happy as when they crammed into the station wagon each summer to go to Walker's Point in Kennebunkport, Maine. "There were five kids, two dogs, Dad in the front passenger seat, and mother driving," said Bush. Walker's Point was named after Mrs. Bush's father, George Herbert Walker. He had bought it as a family vacation home. Grandfather Walker came from St. Louis, Missouri. He studied law and then became a businessman. He was the amateur heavyweight boxing champion of Missouri. An excellent golfer, he was president of the U.S. Golf Association in the early 1920s. Active even as an old man, he taught his grandsons many skills, including fishing and sailing. George Bush was named after his grandfather, and always felt especially close to him.

For the Bush children, Maine in the summer was the best of all possible adventures. They spent long hours looking for starfish and sea urchins and crabs. They picked berries, climbed trees, and hiked in the woods. Nature's bounty was all around them—the wonder of tidal pools, the smell of salt air, the sounds of waves crashing on the rocks at night, summer storms sweeping along the rocky coastline.

Mr. Walker had a sailboat named *Tomboy*. It was a great adventure when he took the children out in deep water to fish. He didn't approve of fancy equipment for the sport. The children used a basic green line that they dropped over the side. And they weren't allowed to use worms or other live bait. A piece of cloth from an old shirt or handkerchief would lure the fish.

"Hooking a big mackerel that put up a good fight," said Bush, "then pulling it in, was pure summertime pleasure. For us kids it ranked right up there with ice cream and staying up late."

Mr. Walker taught the older boys how to handle and dock the boat. When George was nine and Prescott, Jr., eleven, he let them take *Tomboy* out into the Atlantic Ocean by themselves.

"My brother and I still remember that first sea adventure," Bush recalls. "The thrill of doing it on our own. We were

5

excited to do what Grandfather had taught us—how to rig the sails, handle swift currents and tides. That first time out by ourselves a storm blew up. It was sudden and we were knocked around a little. We were scared, but we brought the boat home. The family was on the dock, and everyone looked worried. But Grandfather said he knew we could do it. That gave me confidence that's lasted all my life."

Sailing became one of George Bush's great loves. Handling boats of all kinds became second nature to him. He loved the feeling of controlling a boat in rough water and battering waves. That love of the sea would later influence his choice of military service in World War II.

At fourteen Bush entered Phillips Andover Academy in Andover, Massachusetts. It was one of the best prep schools in the country. In those days schools like Phillips Andover or Groton were strictly for the sons of upper-class families. After graduation the students usually moved on to universities like Yale, Harvard, or Princeton. They went into family businesses, law, banking, or advertising. All their lives they had the same ideas—about social class, making money, and privilege. It was the kind of life that George Bush was meant to live. But he wanted something else for himself!

At Phillips Andover, Bush was one of the most popular boys. He was an excellent student and one of the best athletes. He was active in many school activities. But he was especially loved by the younger students. Bruce Gelb was one of those students.

"I became a political fund raiser only because of one man," Gelb said, "and that's George Bush. At Phillips Andover he was my hero. . . ."

Gelb was a freshman when Bush was a senior. During his second week in school, an older student ordered him to move a big, heavy couch from one end of the hall to the other.

"I dragged and dragged it," Gelb said, "and then I told the guy I couldn't lift it anymore. He grabbed me and put my arm behind my back and began twisting it. I yelled, 'You can break it off—I can't lift it anymore!' "

At that moment a tall boy came into the long hall. He just said, "Leave the kid alone," and kept on walking. The bully instantly dropped Gelb's arm.

"Who was that?" Gelb asked the other boy.

"That was George Bush. He's the greatest guy in school."

Bush graduated that year, but Gelb never forgot him. They didn't meet again until 1978. Gelb still thought of Bush as his schoolboy hero and has raised campaign money for him ever since.

Before Bush graduated from prep school, the Japanese had bombed Pearl Harbor on December 7, 1941. America was in the thick of World War II. He had no doubts about which branch of service he would join. He loved the sea, but he also wanted to fly. He became a Navy pilot. College was coming up in the fall of 1942, but George decided it would have to wait. The sooner he could enlist the better. He was young, patriotic, and felt that serving his country was more important now than attending college.

The speaker at Bush's graduation was Henry Stimson, Secretary of War. He told members of Bush's class of 1942 that the war would be a long one. America needed fighting men, he said, but the graduates would serve their country better by getting more education. After the ceremony Prescott Bush pulled his son aside for a moment.

"George," he said, "did Secretary Stimson say anything to change your mind?"

"No, sir. I'm going in."

On his eighteenth birthday Bush went to Boston, Massachusetts, and was sworn into the Navy as a Seaman Second Class. Soon after, he was headed south for pre-flight training at Chapel Hill, North Carolina. Bush was younger than the other trainees and looked even younger than his age. He was six feet two inches tall, skinny, and, he said, "fuzz-faced and self-conscious."

His decision to enlist won Bush many admirers when he entered politics. The editor of a liberal magazine disliked Bush's conservative outlook through the years. But he wrote:

"Almost all those in the Phillips Andover Class of 1942 went on to college for a year or two or three after graduation. George Bush didn't. He knew what his duty was."

War Hero

At this time, the Navy was short of pilots and cut its training course to ten months. But it was still a long time before Bush climbed into a training plane at the Chapel Hill base. He had the idea that his instructor thought he was too young to be trusted with expensive Navy equipment. But the first time he climbed into the trainer, he felt at home. With his good athlete's reflexes he was quick to learn.

Bush was home for Christmas of 1942 and was invited to a big party. He looked handsome in his uniform, but he was shy and didn't ask any of the girls to dance. He was about to leave when he spotted a very pretty blond girl in a red and green holiday dress. He asked a friend who knew the girl to introduce him to her. Her name was Barbara Pierce, and she lived in Rye, New York. George finally asked her to dance. They were about to walk out on the floor when the band changed to a fast tune. Both started to apologize to the other—neither could dance to the fast swing music. They laughed and sat out the dance—in fact, they *talked* the entire evening away.

It was a meeting right out of a storybook—love at first sight. After Bush returned to training in North Carolina, the two wrote constantly. But fortunately, Barbara was going to school in South Carolina, and she went up to Chapel Hill on many weekends. George was only eighteen, Barbara seventeen. He was afraid his fellow cadets would make fun of him because she was so young, and he begged her to say she was eighteen. Few cadets were aware Bush was so young. He got his wings when he was only eighteen, and was the youngest pilot in the Navy. He took advanced flight training in Corpus Christi, Texas. In August 1943, he and Barbara went to his family's summer home in Maine. They announced their engagement, but knew it might be years before they could marry. They had promised their parents to wait until after the war.

In the fall of 1943 Bush became a bomber pilot aboard the aircraft carrier *San Jacinto*. He flew a Grumman Avenger bomber and nicknamed the plane "Barbara." His crewmen were Jack Delaney, the radioman-tail gunner, and Bill White, the turret gunner. The three men became good friends, and they flew many dangerous missions over Pacific islands held by the Japanese. It was a special kind of friendship—the kind only people who risk their lives together ever experience. They lived through many close calls—but nothing compared to what happened on September 2, 1944, over an enemy island called Chichi Jima.

Bush's Avenger bomber was hit by anti-aircraft fire as he dived on a radio station. "It felt," he said later, "as if a giant fist had crunched into the belly of the plane." The Avenger was on fire and smoke poured into the cockpit. Bush stayed with the dive and dropped four bombs. He headed for open sea and ordered his crewmen to bail out, but he never saw them jump.

The fire was coming close to the cockpit. It was time for Bush to jump. He leaped and pulled the ripcord of his parachute . . . a split-second too soon. His head banged into the side of the bomber, and his parachute almost got caught on the tail. He had a nasty cut on his forehead, but felt himself floating free. When he hit the water, he quickly slipped from the parachute harness, inflated the raft in his seatpack, and climbed in. Suddenly he saw a Japanese boat cutting fast toward him. Two American planes were in the area and fought the boat off. Bush suddenly realized the Japanese were trying to capture him. His heart began to hammer. He had heard horror stories about the enemy often killing downed American pilots. At best, his capture would mean spending the rest of the war in a Japanese prison camp. He looked around for Delaney or White, but couldn't spot them.

A pilot dropped him a medical kit, and he put some medicine on his wound. He checked his .38 pistol and it was working. "But for all the good it would do me," Bush said, "I would have traded fifty pistols for one small paddle." Alone on the empty sea, he saw planes heading back to the carriers. The ships would soon start south— and he was slowly drifting in toward the Japanese island.

Bush paddled hard with his hands. But the strong current kept him in the same place. Where were his friends? They were nowhere in sight. All he saw was vast blue sky and choppy green water. He had been stung by a sea creature and was sick to his stomach from swallowing sea water. Praying the sting wasn't poisonous, he struggled to keep from being pulled into the island. If he wasn't rescued soon, his luck would run out. George tried to keep up his hope, his courage. He wondered what had happened to Delaney and White.

He drifted and paddled for three hours. Suddenly a submarine surfaced only a hundred yards away. Was it an enemy ship? Luck was with him—it was an American ship, the U.S.S. *Finback*. Sailors pulled Bush out of his raft as a submarine officer filmed the rescue. Bush was greeted by three other pilots rescued by the sub. They would have to stay aboard the *Finback* for a month until she finished her combat patrol. Bush silently thanked God for saving his life, and prayed for his crewmen. When he learned, upon leaving the submarine, that neither man had lived, he felt guilty that only he had survived. One went down with the plane. The other was seen jumping, but his parachute failed to open. Six days after his rescue, Bush wrote a letter to his parents that was mailed when the sub again reached port. It described his feelings about the fate of Delaney and White:

". . . I try to think about it as little as possible. Yet I cannot get the thought of those two men out of my mind. Oh, I'm O.K.—I want to fly again and I won't be scared. But I know I won't be able to shake the memory of this incident, and I don't want to completely. . . ."

George made many lifelong friends aboard the *Finback* and came to admire the bravery and skill of the submarine's crew. Twenty years old, he was very young during his time aboard the sub. But his brush with death and the loss of close friends made him do some serious thinking. He searched for answers about life, the future he wanted. He realized he had been given a second chance—and it taught him how to live: *Give life everything you've got. Don't hold back and don't look for the easy way out. Just do what you should do.* He often said that the time aboard the *Finback* was probably the most important of his life.

Bush was awarded the Distinguished Flying Cross for "extraordinary heroism" on his mission over Chichi Jima. He went back to the *San Jacinto* eight weeks after he was shot down. He had flown enough missions to be sent home, but he wanted to stay in combat. He took part in attacks against the Japanese in the Philippine Islands. After flying fifty-eight missions he was ordered home in December 1944.

He was excited about going home for the holiday and thought he and Barbara should get married despite their earlier promise to their parents to wait until the war was over. The war seemed far away during that joyous holiday time. He felt safe surrounded by family and friends and the woman he loved. "It was an unforgettable, happy time for me." But, Bush said, part of him was still out in the Pacific . . . with friends still there . . . friends who were lost.

Together, at Last

There seemed to be no reason for the young couple to wait any longer. On January 6, 1945, George Bush and Barbara Pierce were married in the First Presbyterian Church in Rye, New York. "And for me," Bush said, "it's been one of the world's greatest love stories ever since." A few months later he was ordered to join another bomber squadron in Virginia City, Virginia, and Barbara went with him. The squadron was preparing for the invasion of Japan. "The Pacific war seemed like it was going to stretch forever," Bush said. "Ten of the original fourteen pilots in our squadron had been killed. If I got shot down this time, I'd leave a beautiful young widow." But the war suddenly ended with the atomic bombing of Hiroshima, Japan, on August 6, 1945.

Bush and his wife were living in a small apartment off the base. They were spending a quiet evening at home when they heard shouts in the street. People listening to the radio had just heard President Harry Truman announce the surrender of Japan. It was a scene the Bushes never forgot. They ran outside to join the celebration. People were laughing and crying and shouting, throwing paper, blowing horns, and banging pots. Men and women hugged each other and danced in the streets. George and Barbara slipped away to a little church. He thought about all his friends who had died. He remembers squeezing Barbara's hand, thanking God for letting him see that day. Walking home, Bush and his wife were excited. They had the same feeling as millions of other young men and women at that time—"We were still young, life lay ahead of us, the world was at peace," George said. "It was the best of times."

In the fall of 1945 he entered Yale University to study economics. It was college with a difference. Gone were the light-hearted rah-rah times of before the war. The students were older, more serious.

They were anxio~~ ~~
lives.

The Bushes were cr~~a~~
house that had been cut
tiny apartments for return~~i~~
and their wives. But even t~~h~~
didn't have much space, they fou~~nd that~~
Yale pleasant. Barbara became pre~~gn~~ant,
and George, Jr., was born in July 1946, just
after Bush completed his freshman year.
George was thrilled. He wanted a family, a
big family. He found nothing strange in his
status as father and college student. It was
common in those days.

George shined in sports and studies and
was one of the most popular students. He
was captain of the baseball team and its first
baseman and also played varsity soccer. Yale
had never been a baseball power. But Bush
twice led it to the National Collegiate
championship game. They lost both times,
but he left a strong impression on rival
coaches. Rod Dedeaux was coach of the
University of Southern California team that
beat Yale in 1948:

George Bush very well as ... He was an excellent fielder and ...ugh at bat. I'd put him on my all-time opponent team—which means he was pretty good."

On March 23, 1948, Babe Ruth, the famous baseball player, was honored at a ceremony at Yale. As captain of Yale's baseball team, George Bush had the privilege of greeting him. It was one of the greatest days of George's young life.

Bush was selected for Phi Beta Kappa (the highest academic honor). He was no intellectual, a classmate said, "but a hard worker who got an 'A' in most courses." Bush was a young man in a hurry; he had a family to support. "I needed my degree to go into the business world as soon as possible." Most Yale graduates in those days went into business or the professions. Bush could have gone into banking with his father. He didn't know exactly what he wanted to do—but he knew what he didn't want. He hated the idea of a nine to five office job and living in the suburbs. He had come of age in a time of war. He had seen different kinds of people and the way they lived. He had experienced danger and the loss of friends. In his autobiography, *Looking Forward,* Bush spoke of his thoughts at that time:

"The world I'd known before the war didn't interest me. I was looking for a different kind of life. I wanted something exciting and challenging. Barbara had the same feeling—that life should be an adventure. If we were going to break away from the life we'd grown up in, we had to do it on our own."

They never thought of asking their families for a loan. Bush had saved three thousand dollars in the Navy. It was enough money to get them started. They were still in their early twenties and wanted to make their own way—even make their own mistakes. He thought of applying for a Rhodes Scholarship to Oxford University in England. But it would mean another year in school. He'd lost three years in the war, and he didn't think it was the right move. He and Barbara thought of starting a farm. But when they discovered how much it would cost to start one, they decided against it. When he graduated from Yale in June 1949, a friend of his father's named Neil Mallon offered him a job.

"What you need to do," Mallon said, "is head out to Texas and the oil fields. That's the place for ambitious young people today. I've got a company in West Texas called Ideco. We supply everything to drill for oil. There's a place for a trainee, an equipment clerk. There's not much salary to start. But if you want to learn the oil business, that's the place."

At first it didn't sound like much to Bush. He thought—*Why bury myself in a dull job in a strange place?* But he quickly realized that he had to be more practical. Mallon was giving him a chance to do something really different with his life. He had to make a fast decision. After talking it over with Barbara, they decided to gamble on Texas. Bush suddenly felt his future was tied up with the state. He had taken advanced flight training in Texas. His carrier was named *San Jacinto* and flew the Lone Star flag of Texas. San Jacinto was where Texans won a great victory over the Mexicans in their fight for freedom. He told Mallon he'd take the job.

He said good-by to his wife and son and started for Odessa, Texas, in the red Studebaker he had bought in college. He was to find a place for the family to live and get a start on the job. Barbara and their son would follow as soon as he made arrangements. He was lonesome on the trip to Texas, and the farther west he drove in the state, the more depressed he became. It was hot, windy, barren country with tumbleweeds and few trees. The heat was unbearable. But he kept telling himself— *underneath that worthless soil is a fortune in oil, and I'm going to take my shot at it.*

Bush was shocked when he drove into Odessa. He knew what industrial towns looked like back East. But he'd never seen a town that looked like one big equipment yard. The oil business was booming. There were oil drills everywhere. Americans were back on wheels after the war. Each year there were more cars on the road. Oil was needed to produce gasoline for these cars.

Bush headed for the Ideco store. It was a large, tin-roofed, one-story building. Inside, it was crammed to the ceiling with heavy equipment.

Bush found a place to live and after a week on the job sent for Barbara and his son. The small house was divided into two apartments by a thin wall. The Bushes had a bedroom and small kitchen and shared the bathroom with their noisy neighbors. There was an old air conditioner that did little to cool the burning Texas summer. But once they were settled, George and Barbara never regretted the move. Their friends back East might have beautiful homes and good jobs. But they were excited about their new life. They felt like pioneers.

Out West

Bush knew he had to prove himself quickly at Ideco. The men he worked with were tough, no-nonsense types. They had lived hard all their lives. They wondered what Bush, an eastern college boy, was doing there. But Bush worked hard to have them accept him. He learned the company's equipment and asked a lot of questions about drilling for oil. This was a new life for him, and he would do whatever he was asked, even sweep the floor. He wanted no special treatment, and the other men accepted him.

The job meant long hours away from his family. But even when he had a few hours off, there was little to do in Odessa for entertainment. It was a rough western town with only two small movie theaters that showed mostly westerns. There was no stage theater, music concerts, or even decent restaurants.

But he and Barbara didn't care. They were too busy becoming Texans. He developed a love for chicken-fried steak, a steak fried in batter. Forty years later it is still one of his favorite foods. They made friends with a few young couples and had Sunday barbecues after church. Little by little they threw off much of their eastern lives and became true Texans.

They were both sports fans, but they never saw anything like Texas football fever. To Texans, football was next in importance to their religion. The weekly high school game was the big event. The Bushes became great fans of the local team. Every Friday night they went to a game. They cheered for the Odessa "Broncos" against rivals like Abilene, Midland, or San Angelo. "And I cheered as hard for them as I ever did for Yale against Harvard," Bush said.

Every workday morning Bush joined oilmen at Nell's Diner for coffee. They talked about the oil business and kept up on the local gossip. George was a hard worker and didn't remain an equipment clerk for long.

He was soon promoted to the job of assemblyman—the worker who put different parts of equipment together. Because he handled steel parts, he had to become a member of the United Steelworkers Union. Bush worked so hard and showed so much promise, he was again promoted, this time to salesman of drilling bits. The bit is the sharpest part of the drill that bores into the earth. He drove long distances to oil drillers near towns with names like Muleshoe, Pecos, and No Trees. It was an important job. He had to know what size bits his customers needed and what kind of rock they were drilling into.

Bush was impressed by the "wildcatters" in the oil fields. They were the men who put up the money to drill for oil. They were gamblers. Every time they spent money to drill, they took a chance. If the well came up dry, they lost money. But if they struck oil, they were suddenly rich. Bush knew that was what he wanted to do—take the chance. Even more than the money, he wanted the adventure. He didn't know enough yet about oil drilling to leave Ideco. But now he would never be content with just selling equipment.

While he thought about going out on his own, Bush became one of Ideco's top salesmen. There were new oil strikes in California, and the company transferred him there to open new territory. The family lived in many places as Bush followed the oil strikes—Bakersfield, Whittier, Centura, and Compton, where their first daughter, Robin, was born in 1949. She was a beautiful, blond, hazel-eyed child, and was adored by her parents.

Bush's routine was always the same. He led the hard life of a salesman on the road, living out of a suitcase and sleeping in cheap motels or in his car. Every day he'd load up the car with drill bits and drive a hundred miles up to the oil fields in rugged country. He drove at least a thousand miles a week. George did so well in California, the company sent him to Midland, Texas. Despite the pleasant living in California, the Bushes now truly thought of Texas as their home. Their lives in the

East were becoming a distant memory.

Returning to Texas was wonderful, but the transfer to Midland was especially exciting. Midland was the biggest oil boomtown of them all. The first great oil strike happened there in 1922. By the end of the 1920s it was called the oil capital of West Texas.

Because oil was needed for planes and tanks and military vehicles, great fortunes were made in Midland during World War II. When Bush arrived there, it was becoming a bustling city of skyscrapers and was soon known as the Tall City of the Plains.

Many bright, hard-working young people had also come to Midland from all over the country. The Bushes settled into a pleasant new house. The future looked bright in Midland during the early 1950s.

"The money could be made quickly," said Bush, "but it wasn't easy. We were young in the business, but had enough experience to know that much. It would take energy and hard work—and, of course, a little luck."

The oil business was exciting, but there were drawbacks to living in a boomtown. People had only oil and fast money on their minds. They worked in oil and talked about oil—and dreamed of striking it rich.

"The first thing a man in the oil business needed," Bush said, "was an understanding wife. We worked long hours, and they spent a lot of time alone with the children."

Most of the wives had come to the West Texas plains from big cities. They were well-educated young women and found little to do in Midland. Later there would be a symphony orchestra, a theater, improved libraries, and good restaurants. But in the early days the big event of the week, as in Odessa, was the Sunday cookout. It was a typical American scene. There were kids playing, dogs barking, food cooking on the grill, a pickup softball or touch football game. George and Barbara made many good friends in those years. But as pleasant as life was, George felt uneasy.

He was making a good salary now. There was a chance he could become an executive in the company. But he was bored with the routine. Every morning he went to the Ideco office, then returned home tired after a very long day. Much of the time he was on the road and away from his family. At the end of the week there was a paycheck, but for the little time he saw Barbara and his children, he might as well have stayed back East and gone into banking. He had come to Texas for more than this kind of life. It was exactly what he had wanted to escape when he left college.

George decided he would become an independent oil operator—a wildcatter. It was a better way to be part of the excitement than selling equipment for Ideco. He wanted to take a risk—go into business for himself. He wondered how Neil Mallon would take his quitting. Ideco had spent a long time training him during the two and a half years he had been with the company, and now his experience was valuable. But he was determined to make the move.

Mr. Mallon did say he was sorry to see George go, but then he surprised George when he said he would do the same thing in his place. Not only that, but he told George exactly how to go about reaching his goal.

Mallon took out a yellow pad and started writing. In the next hour Bush got a crash course in how to form and finance his company. He left Mallon's office with a load off his shoulders. But he knew the real trial lay ahead. In just a few weeks there would be no steady paycheck. And he had a wife and two children to support. When he talked to Barbara about his concerns, she encouraged him to make the break: "That's why we came to Texas."

George went into business with John Overby, a neighbor and friend. Their company was called Bush-Overby Oil Development. The two men were sure they could make a success of the business. They began by buying the rights to drill for oil on land owned by farmers and ranchers. The land owner was paid a sum of money before any drilling was done. If oil was found on the land, Bush-Overby made money. If no oil was found, the company lost money, because they had already paid the farmer or rancher.

Like most people in business for themselves, Bush worked twice as hard as he did at Ideco. He now had the responsibility to make decisions which could make or break the company. On the road much more than when he was a salesman, he drove long distances and was tired and lonely much of the time. But he never found his new business dull. One day he might be out on a dusty road heading to a ranch. The next night he might be flying to New York or Chicago looking for investors, people who could offer money to keep the business going. He still didn't want to go to his family for a loan.

In March 1951 there was an oil strike in North Dakota. Bush and his partner wanted to get there fast to buy drilling rights. The experience was typical of Bush's roving, exciting life at the time. He had a neighbor who was a former Navy pilot and owned a small plane. Bush and Overby were flown to Minot, North Dakota. Then they had to take a freezing ride in an open jeep to the county office where the land records were kept. The records told them who owned which parcels of land.

They did almost no business. Mobil—a major oil company—had men in North Dakota before Bush and Overby got there, and they bought up the best land for drilling.

But the worst part of the North Dakota trip was the plane ride home. The pilot figured he could make it nonstop back to Midland, Texas. But the weather was rough, and the temperature kept dropping. Ice formed on the wings, and the small plane had no de-icing equipment. The situation grew worse as they ran through a heavy snowstorm. They hit clear weather for a few miles, then a thunderstorm rolled in. The pilot found a small opening in the clouds and landed way off course at Miles City, Montana. Bush said that he was never this scared during the war, even with the enemy firing at him.

Everyone in the oil business seemed to be making money. But Bush-Overby was just getting by. Bush, however, never questioned his decision to leave Ideco. It was only a matter of time . . . sticking to it . . . giving it his best. That had always been his way. But he had many sleepless nights. He knew the company's troubles came from a lack of money to expand. Big money was the only way to make bigger money in the oil business. The days of the grizzled old wildcatter striking it rich alone were gone.

Suddenly Bush had a stroke of luck. Two brothers, Hugh and Bill Licdtke, suggested a partnership. They would raise $500,000, and Bush-Overby would raise the same amount. One million dollars would give the new company, Zapata Petroleum, a good stake to develop their oil drilling. Bush figured it was the right move—and it had come at the right time. But he couldn't raise his share of the partnership on his own, and finally had to go to his family for a loan. His father and an uncle loaned him the money. The future for Bush and his partners seemed bright. Then tragedy struck the family.

Daughter Robin had seemed tired for weeks. She rarely played like other children, and ate poorly. No one was alarmed, but the Bush's family doctor, Dorothy Wyvell, had Robin admitted to the Midland hospital for tests. One day Bush was checking land records in a town far from Midland when Barbara called him. Her voice sounded urgent, and she told him to return home immediately. He hurried home and drove right to the hospital. Doctor Wyvell had difficulty talking—and Bush sensed there was something seriously wrong with Robin. Finally Doctor Wyvell gave them the bad news. She had run tests on Robin. Their little girl was very sick. She had leukemia, a form of cancer. Bush quickly asked what could be done. The doctor's answer stunned him:

"Nothing. The disease has spread all over her body. She has only a short time to live. It might be a few weeks . . . maybe a few days."

The doctor said the best thing was to take Robin home, make her as comfortable as possible—let nature take its course. Little was known about leukemia in those days. But the Bushes weren't going to give up their daughter without a fight. George called his uncle, Dr. John Walker, a cancer specialist at Memorial Hospital in New York. Walker said they were doing research into leukemia and urged Bush to bring Robin to New York.

"Don't get your hopes too high," he warned. "Maybe nothing can be done. We're just beginning our research. But even if the odds are a million to one, you've got to give life a chance."

The Bushes knew they would never forgive themselves if they didn't do everything possible to help their daughter. They flew to New York with Robin, and she was admitted to the hospital. Barbara was always at her bedside. George flew back and forth to Midland after the first few weeks. In the next six months there were times when Robin seemed perfectly healthy. But George had prepared himself for the worst. Despite periods of improvement, doctors said not to get their hopes up. Robin, age three years and ten months, held on desperately to life. Bush and his wife prayed, but when Robin died, he said,

"It was our faith that truly helped us, kept us going. Gradually but surely Robin slipped away."

Years later he wrote in his auto-biography:

"To this day, like every parent who has lost a child—we wonder why. Yet we know that whatever the reason, she is in God's loving arms."

"It brought us much closer together," Barbara said. "Many families are shattered by the same experience. Afterward George was unbelievable. He was so strong. He held me in his arms a lot and let me weep."

Five-year-old George plays in the snow.

Even at age 17, George Bush, seated second from the left, showed signs of leadership. He was a member of the Student Council at Phillips Academy.

George, the youngest pilot in the Navy, won medals for his heroism.

George and Barbara dance at their wedding.

At Yale, George greets baseball great, Babe Ruth.

A family portrait—Standing (left to right): Neil, Jeb, and George, Jr. On the sofa with their parents: Dorothy and Marvin.

In 1974, George traveled to China.

C.I.A. Director George Bush traveled to Georgia to meet with Jimmy Carter in 1976.

Presidential candidate Ronald Reagan and his running mate, George Bush, wave to reporters in front of the nation's Capitol in 1980.

Vice President Bush and Barbara visit the Sphinx in Cairo, Egypt, during an official visit in 1986.

El Koussy/SYGMA

SYGMA

Presidential hopeful George Bush campaigns in New Hampshire in February 1988.

46

George Bush and his running mate, Dan Quayle, acknowledge their supporters at the Republican National Convention on August 18, 1988.

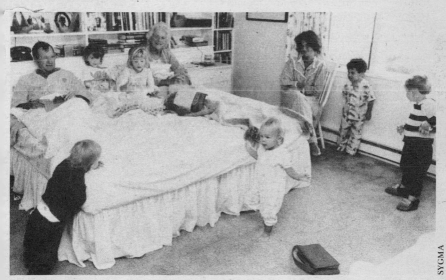

George and Barbara always make time for their grandchildren.

The forty-first President and the First Lady.

New Challenges

By the age of thirty George Bush had already gone through more than most men do in a lifetime. He had lost good friends in the war and still felt some guilt about it. He had nearly lost his life in combat. He had taken a chance and built a business by tireless work. He had lost his only daughter. But Bush kept his unhappiness to himself. He was an old-fashioned man in that sense.

It took Bush a long time to refocus his attention on the oil business after Robin's death. But he knew that hard work was the best cure for his grief.

The new oil company Bush-Overby had formed with the Liedtke brothers was lucky from the beginning. By 1954 it had 71 wells bringing in thousands of barrels of oil a day. A few years later the company had 127 productive wells. The Liedtke brothers were satisfied with their business.

But Bush and Overby wanted to try making money by taking oil from beneath the seas and oceans—offshore drilling. At this point the four-man partnership split. The Liedtkes stayed with land drilling; George and Overby turned to the sea. Their first task, and major expense, was paying someone to build a new kind of offshore drilling rig. It was like a three-legged steel and concrete island in the ocean. The three giant legs were driven into the floor of a deep body of water.

Each rig cost three million dollars. A hurricane destroyed their first rig, but Bush insisted they carry on. By 1959 the company had four rigs to dig for oil in deep water. Bush kept watch on the actual drilling. At first they drilled in the Gulf of Mexico and found large deposits of oil. Their business boomed. They expanded their drilling to oceans and seas the world over—in search of still more oil.

Bush's business wasn't the only thing that had grown in 1959. Houston, Texas, now a big city and the financial center for the oil industry, seemed the perfect place for Bush to move his growing family. There were now five children—George, Jr., thirteen; Jeb, seven; Neil, six; Marvin, three; and Dorothy, one. Bush's office was in one of the new skyscrapers. He was a kind, generous boss, but he had one strict rule for his staff. If any of his children called, they were to be put through to him instantly, no matter what he was doing. He was a busy man, but never so busy he couldn't help or advise his children. He prized the precious time on weekends when the family was together.

They now lived in a beautiful home, and had financial security. There was plenty of money for the children's future education. George was still young, only in his mid-thirties when he began to think about new challenges. He became interested in public service and wanted to follow his father into politics. During most of his years in Texas, Bush had worked hard to build up the Republican party in Texas. His father was a Republican, George came from a Republican tradition, and he wanted to break the Democratic hold on Texas voters. But he was still undecided about running for office. He recently had a bitter taste of rough Texas politics, when he witnessed the way oil companies tried to influence politicians.

The big Texas oil companies also produced natural gas. It is a by-product of oil drilling and is used to heat homes and for cooking. Prices for natural gas were being decided by the government. Congress was about to vote on a bill that would change that by allowing the oil companies to set their own prices. Bush thought it was a good bill—it would increase the supply of gas and lower the price. But his father didn't like the bill. Prescott Bush believed it would mean higher gas prices for people in Connecticut, and he spoke out against it.

Both father and son had great pressure put on them. Some oil people asked Bush to convince his father to change his mind. He was warned that his career in politics would be over before it began if he didn't. Others made calls to Bush's former boss, Neil Mallon. The head of Phillips Petroleum, a giant company, told Mallon: "If

Prescott Bush doesn't vote for our bill, you can forget about selling us more equipment. And you can tell George Bush to forget about his offshore drilling business."

Bush received phone calls late at night. The callers threatened to run him out of business if his father didn't "vote right." The calls made him angry—angry enough to do just what his opponents dreaded. Bush was no longer undecided about going into politics. If he was going to change anything—like the threats and pressure of the natural gas affair—he had to be an insider, try to get elected to Congress.

George talked to friends about Texas politics. They advised him to join the Democratic Party. The Democrats ruled Texas politics and had since the Civil War. They said if he switched parties, he'd have a real chance for a U.S. Senate seat. But he'd never get elected as a Republican. Bush, however, was stubborn. He was a Republican and didn't want to switch parties—or his ideas about government.

Not only was George sure that he could convert a new generation of Texas Democrats to the Republican party, but he also saw signs that solid Democratic rule in Texas was showing cracks. John Tower, a conservative Republican, had won a Senate seat. In 1960 Republican Richard Nixon got more votes in Texas than Democrat John F. Kennedy, even though Nixon lost that presidential election.

Bush served as chairman of the local Republican party. He and Barbara were on the road every night talking to people. He worked hard and his message began to get through. In 1964 he became the Republican candidate for U.S. senator from Texas. His opponent was a liberal Democrat, Ralph Yarborough, who was up for re-election.

Bush's chances looked slim. Yarborough was popular, and he had the support of President Lyndon B. Johnson, a Texan, who had become President after John F. Kennedy was assassinated. It would be a political blow to Johnson if his home state had two Republican senators. Bush was not well known outside of Houston, Midland, and Odessa. Important Republicans like Richard Nixon and Barry Goldwater came to Texas to support him. The race got tighter. For a time it looked as if Bush might win. But Yarborough beat him. George Bush learned a valuable lesson from the defeat. There was only one way to succeed in politics. He had to work at it full-time, give it all his energy and dedication. He resigned from Zapata Petroleum in 1966. It wasn't a hard decision for Bush to make. He was more fascinated by politics now than the oil business. And he felt that there were more important things in life than making money. Public service was a way to make a better state, a better country. He sold his shares in Zapata for $1.1 million. Less than two years later they were worth twice as much. If he had stayed in offshore drilling, he would have become very, very rich.

Bush gave up his oil business. But he kept close ties with his long-time friends. Oil men have been the most important fund raisers and supporters of Bush's political campaigns. Two of his sons are now in the oil business. Bush fought many battles for the oil industry during his years in Washington, but he denied "taking sides."

"If you know something about a problem in a business, you shouldn't have to keep silent just because you were once in the business. I sold out my oil interests just so cynical people couldn't make the charge against me that I was in it to feather my own nest."

Bush ran for office again in the 1966 race for the House of Representatives. His opponent this time was a conservative Democrat. Their views were much the same, and it looked like a tight race. But Bush easily defeated his opponent. In his first term as a congressman, George showed real political courage with regard to an issue that concerned black people.

An open housing bill came before Congress in April 1968. This law would allow people—of any race—to live where they wanted. The country was going through the civil rights struggle. Black people, and white people who supported them, wanted to strike down all bars to voting, housing, jobs, and education. Blacks wanted their full rights as American citizens. Martin Luther King, Jr., the great civil rights leader, was killed that month in Memphis, Tennessee. There were riots in cities all around the country.

Bush was a conservative, but he was always very liberal about human rights. He knew his vote on the open housing bill was very important. He received many letters from his Texas district telling him to vote against the bill. Though he risked his political future, George stayed true to his beliefs and voted *for* the bill. After the vote his office was swamped with hate mail, and he received death threats. Bush knew he could ride out the storm if he stayed in Washington, but that's not what he wanted to do! He wanted to speak to the people back home in Texas—especially the people who were against the bill.

The open housing bill had become law, and a week after the vote Bush flew home to Houston. The meeting place was jammed with people. There were boos and jeers when Bush was introduced. He didn't want to get into a shouting contest. There was only one way to explain his vote. He had to explain to his audience what being their congressman meant. He waited calmly until the audience gave him a chance to speak. Without any excuses, he began:

"Your representative in Congress owes you not only his hard work—but his judgment. If I sacrifice it to your opinion, I betray you—instead of serving you."

He said that was the way he saw his job as congressman. But there was something just as important—even if his all-white audience disagreed. The housing bill deserved their support, he said, just as well as his.

"At this very minute many black Americans are fighting and dying in Vietnam. How would you feel if such a man came home to be denied the freedom other Americans have? . . . A man shouldn't have a door slammed in his face because he is black, or speaks with a Latin American accent. Open housing offers hope to blacks and other minorities. They have been locked out too long by habit and discrimination."

As Bush talked, the audience grew silent. The boos and rude shouts stopped. When he finished talking, he looked out on row after row of silent faces. He thought he had failed to get his message across. But as he started for his seat, the applause began. It grew louder and louder. The crowd stood and kept up the thunderous clapping. The ugliness that had gone before had vanished. Bush sensed that something special had happened. Right there—because of what he said—people had had a change of heart.

"To this day," he said, "nothing in my long political life thrilled me like that."

George Bush learned that a politician *could* improve things. He *could* make the country a better place. It taught him the most valuable lesson of all—trust the goodness and intelligence of the average person.

Bush was re-elected in 1968, the year Richard Nixon was elected President. He had his sights set on 1970 to make another run against Ralph Yarborough for senator. Yarborough's liberal record was now opposed by many Texas Democrats. Bush thought he could get those Democratic votes. He also knew that former President Lyndon B. Johnson did not like Yarborough. Johnson lived in Texas and was still a great power in Texas politics.

But George had no way of knowing what Johnson had up his sleeve. Johnson pushed Yarborough aside for a more attractive candidate, Lloyd Bentsen. Bentsen was a forty-eight-year-old conservative Democrat and wealthy Houston businessman. Bush gave up his House seat and entered the race for senator. He received over a million votes—and lost. He returned to Washington to serve out his last weeks in Congress. Reporters asked him how he felt, and what the future held for him:

"After you get over the initial hurt, the blow of losing, it's not so bad," Bush replied. "The future doesn't look nearly as gloomy as it did eight hours ago."

He received a disturbing letter from a Texas man:

I did not vote for you . . . because as a congressman you had voted for the "Open Housing

Law." A lot of people I know didn't vote for you either . . . Maybe they have you still pegged as a Connecticut Yankee just as I do.

Bush quickly replied:

You have me pegged as a Connecticut Yankee. I have you pegged as a mean bigot. Gosh, it feels good to get things off my chest like this.

It made him feel better, but he didn't know what to do next. He could run for Congress again in 1972, but that didn't seem smart. He would be starting over again as a freshman congressman with no power. He was forty-six years old and retired from business. Now he was a failed politician. But because he had been such a loyal Republican, someone would come to his rescue.

Many Jobs

It was President Nixon who had asked Bush to run for office. After Bush's defeat, the President felt that Bush should be rewarded for party loyalty. Bush, however, told Nixon that the decision to run was his own. He had run because he wanted to, not because of anyone's influence. But the President insisted. He told Bush that he was too valuable to sit on the sidelines. He named Bush to be United States Ambassador to the United Nations (U.N.), and the family moved to New York City. He was sure Bush's political experience would help.

There were newspaper editorials for and against Bush's appointment:

The *Washington Star:* "By naming a congressman who was a 'political loser,' a man with no experience in foreign affairs or diplomacy—Nixon has downgraded the United Nations."

The *New York Times:* "There seems to be

nothing in his record that qualifies him for this highly important position."

The *Pittsburgh Post-Gazette:* "The President has found a man with interest and capacity to fill an important job with distinction."

The criticism made George anxious to meet the challenge before him. He wanted to prove his critics wrong. Though he had been a strong supporter of the United Nations when it was created in 1945, by the early 1970s, his opinion had changed. He no longer thought of the U.N. as the best hope for peace. It did little to settle important political matters. Still, it made many advances in science, medicine, agriculture, space technology, and the welfare of the world's children. Bush took up his U.N. post in March 1971.

"I had no illusions about the limitations of the United Nations. Or about my role as Amcrica's representative . . . I was there to support my country's policies—not to apologize for them."

These were very tense times at the U.N. Bush often had to act as peacemaker between the Arabs and Israelis. He tried not to show favor to either side. In one incident the Russians were brought into the fight. Shots were fired into the Russian embassy. A member of the Jewish Defense League was arrested. Rabbi Meir Kahane, the organization's leader, stopped Bush in the U.N. building: "Why won't you talk to me? All I want is a dialogue."

Bush was very angry and replied, "Because I've seen your idea of a dialogue—those shots fired at the Russians. I don't condone your group's violence any more than the violence directed at Jews in Israel by Arab terrorists!"

George often felt bitter and disgusted as he watched the constant fighting between nations. But he never let his personal feelings show. He was well-liked by everyone at the U.N., even the representatives from anti-American countries. One time he risked his friendship with other U.N. officials. In the 1972 Olympic Games eleven Israeli athletes were killed by Arab terrorists. Israel then made attacks on terrorist strongholds. Much to Bush's disgust, the U.N.

wanted to condemn only Israel. He voted against it.

"Some of the Arab ambassadors were my friends," Bush said. "When I voted against condemning Israel, one Arab said he'd never shake my hand again. I told him I wasn't going to leave the room until we shook hands. We argued and there were angry words. But we shook hands and were friends again."

George Bush always liked to settle matters with talk. It sometimes made people think he was weak, but he felt this ability was one of his greatest strengths.

"I believe you can win—in life or politics—without making enemies. I like to persuade people, not fight with them."

More trouble was ahead for Bush at the United Nations. Acting on President Nixon's order, he fought hard to keep Communist China out of the U.N. Meanwhile, Nixon was secretly acting to improve relations between the two countries. Bush was asked if he didn't feel that Nixon had made a fool of him.

"No," he said. "The President manages

foreign policy any way he wants. Sometimes he has to keep his purposes secret from those working for him. I was working for Nixon then. I did my best. He wanted to go another way. I understand that."

In 1972 Nixon was re-elected. He sent for Bush, who was still at the United Nations.

"George, I need you for another tough job," the President said. "I want you to be chairman of the National Republican Party (N.R.P.). This is an important time for Republicans. We have a chance to make the party even more powerful in the next four years. I think you're the man who can do it."

Bush agreed to take the job. The family moved to Washington from New York. "It was back to life in the political fast lane," he said.

He was once again at the center of power. But soon after this appointment, Richard Nixon was forced to resign as President. Some men working for Nixon's campaign staff had broken into the National Democratic Party headquarters at the Watergate Hotel in Washington, D.C., to steal information. Nixon and his top advisers tried to keep the break-in secret. This was against the law. The Congress and the people of the United States couldn't allow a president who had disobeyed the country's laws to remain in office and Richard Nixon resigned.

In the beginning, Bush was loyal to Nixon and defended him. But by August 1973, he felt that Nixon should resign from the Presidency. If he stayed, he would ruin the Republican party. He wrote Nixon a letter:

"I now feel your resignation is best for the country. This view is held by most Republican leaders. This letter is very difficult because of the gratitude I will always feel toward you. . . . "

It was the hardest thing Bush ever had to do in politics. He wrote the letter, he said, "because a political party and the country are bigger and more important than any one person, even a President." He was sad because he saw Nixon's downfall as a tragedy. But what had happened was Nixon's business. Bush did his job and held the Republican Party together.

After Nixon resigned, Vice President Gerald Ford became President. He invited Bush to the White House to talk about his role in the new administration. Bush wasn't sure what he wanted to do next. His job as N.R.P. chairman had been very difficult. Bush and his wife liked living in Washington. But now they were ready to get away from politics in the capital—if the right job came along.

President Ford said there were two prize ambassador jobs open. One in France, the other in Great Britain. They were the most glamorous, most popular jobs. American ambassadors in those countries lived very comfortable lives and had much leisure time. They lived in two of the great cities of the world. There was little work except routine diplomatic tasks and attending ceremonies to honor dignataries.

George Bush had something else in mind. He knew the American envoy in

China was leaving. He told President Ford he wanted that job. Ford was surprised, but Bush convinced him. Later, Bush would answer his critics who said he always had things too easy. He said he always chose the difficult, challenging job.

"I could have gone to London or Paris and lived in luxury, with the limousine and tennis court and big house and servants. I chose Beijing. It was the future."

He had talked with Barbara before he met with the President. Like their decision to go to Texas, they welcomed the appointment to China *because* of the difficult challenge it presented. They'd go together if Bush could get the job. It would be an exciting journey into the unknown. China's Communist rulers had kept the country out of contact with the West for many years. And America and China were not on good terms with each other. A friend of Bush's in the State Department couldn't understand his decision.

"Yes, China is very important," he told Bush, "and there might be some serious work there. But you'll find the Chinese leaders will try to stop you at every turn. For the most part you'll be bored out of your head."

George and Barbara Bush left for Beijing, China, in September 1974. Their children stayed in the United States, some in school, the younger ones cared for by relatives. After his first weeks in China, Bush began to think his State Department friend was right. But he set out to make his job more important. He knew the first thing to do was to try and get close to the Chinese people.

With time, the Bushes loved China. They stopped using the embassy car and rode bicycles like ordinary citizens. They became known to the Chinese as "Bushers, who ride bicycles, just as Chinese do." They traveled around the country and saw the fabled sights, the Great Wall, and the magnificent temples. Barbara Bush was fascinated by the people and their culture. She studied Chinese history, art, and architecture. The couple was respected and loved by the Chinese.

The Bushes worked hard to develop trust between the U.S. and China, but at first Bush found it hard to deal with the Chinese leaders, who were often very secretive and suspicious of Americans. One high official, however, was a good friend of Bush's from their days together at the United Nations. With his help, Bush was able to make some progress in international relations. "It was no major breakthrough," he said, "but we were able to make things a little easier between the two countries."

The Bush children visited China in the summer of 1975. Daughter Dorothy celebrated her sixteenth birthday in the country, and plans were made to have her baptized. Her baptism had been delayed for years for one reason or another. George and Barbara decided now would be the perfect time. Communist China was officially an atheist country. Its traditional religions—Buddhism, Confucianism, Taoism—were discouraged, as was Chinese Christianity. But the Bushes located a Christian church in Beijing whose minister was willing to baptize Dorothy. When she left the church after the ceremony, the minister said, "We will always love you and always miss you." He told her that she would be a lifelong member of the small church in a Communist land.

After a little more than a year in China, President Ford offered Bush the position of director of the Central Intelligence Agency (C.I.A.). The Bushes found it hard to leave the Orient, but George had to make a quick decision once the offer was made. Though he had doubts about taking the new job, his sense of patriotic duty drove him to accept. He and Barbara flew back to America with warm memories of their time in China. But during the flight home, Bush wondered if he'd made the right move.

His first interest was politics and he still had ambitions to run for office, but the C.I.A. was no springboard to higher office. As head of the agency, he couldn't be directly involved in politics. He had to treat both Republicans and Democrats fairly, and could not be involved in the country's domestic affairs. His only responsibility was to insure America's security against any threat from other countries.

Bush was coming to the agency at a bad time. It was under attack by the press. The C.I.A. was accused of doing illegal things and using too much secrecy to cover up their activities.

Bush wanted to change the bad press stories about the C.I.A. He made public many successful operations that were secret until then. Slowly he began to change the agency's image. He stated that few C.I.A. employees actually did what most people think of as "spy" work. Most of them were specialists who studied foreign countries— their politics, economics, military, agriculture, and science. At least fourteen hundred had masters and doctoral degrees from the best universities. But, he insisted, the agency had to have more agents overseas. And it had to keep secret the way it gathered information.

But for all the good he did, Bush found the director's job frustrating. He spent more time fighting the agency's critics than directing its operations. The job also changed his personal life. He couldn't attend any social event that had to do with politics. But in Washington everything was politics. He could no longer talk about his work with Barbara. He was proud of the job he did, but he wanted to get back to the political arena.

So in 1976, when Jimmy Carter, a Democrat, was elected President, George Bush thought it was a good time to resign. First Bush gave the new President an update on what the C.I.A. was doing to maintain America's security. Then Bush made plans to leave Washington.

Bush was out of a job, but he wouldn't be at loose ends for very long.

A Loss and a Win

In 1977 George Bush returned to private life in Houston. He didn't know what direction to take at first. But when he read about the Republicans who had their eye on the 1980 presidential election, he thought: *What do they have to offer the country that I don't?* He felt none of the men could match his experience.

By that time he had been in government for more than ten years. He had served in many kinds of jobs— Congress, United Nations, Republican National Party, China, Central Intelligence Agency. He'd seen the inner workings of the White House serving two presidents. And he had his own ideas about how the presidency should be run, and what it meant. Someone was needed who believed in the American system and had faith in the people. As time passed, he was sure that Jimmy Carter would not be re-elected. Bush believed he had a very good chance to become President. He decided to run and began building an organization. By the middle of 1978 he was already campaigning.

Bush officially announced himself as a candidate on May 1, 1979. He knew he had to do well in the early primary elections. Primaries are held by Republicans and Democrats to choose or nominate the candidate who will represent the party in the national election. Bush's basic campaign speech began, "I was shot down at twenty. I guess that's not much of a recommendation"—he paused for laughs—"but maybe it's not so bad. It's something to be out there all alone, when you know the country is behind you, united in a great cause." He said the country had serious problems, but its national spirit would pull it through. He felt good about the future. He boldly said that he was the best candidate in the field—because of his government and business experience. "I happen to be the only Republican candidate who built a business and had to meet a payroll." His campaign slogan said he would be "A President We Won't Have to Train."

His chief rival in the primaries was Ronald Reagan. During the campaign, Bush called Reagan weak and too old. In Iowa, Bush pulled off a great upset and beat Reagan. It made him the front-runner for the Republican presidential nomination.

Political experts said Bush wasn't giving Republican voters "a vision for the future." Bush did talk about the direction he wanted to lead the country. But everything he said and stood for was lost as the media talked only about his race with Reagan. He received good advice from Jim Rhodes, a former governor of Ohio. Bush told him the inspirational things he'd said to voters. Rhodes leaned back in his chair.

"George, if you're serious about running for President, you might as well get a few things straight. What you're talking about is dandy. But I want to show you what people vote for, what they *really* want to know." He pulled out a thick wallet from his pocket and slammed it on the table. "That's it right there. Jobs. Which man put money in people's pockets—you or the other guy. That's what it's all about, George—*jobs, jobs, jobs!*"

Bush began to talk about jobs—often slamming his wallet down as Rhodes had done. He kept the campaign going but he was sometimes too innocent. He thought he could be absolutely honest with the voters. If he didn't know the answer to a question, he said so. One time a woman asked him about a situation in the Mideast. Bush said he didn't know the situation. The woman said, "You *don't know*? And you want to *run* American foreign policy?"

One night Bush heard the news—Ronald Reagan had won enough votes in Nebraska to make him the Republican candidate. But Bush had won many votes. The Republicans wanted the strongest possible ticket. That's why Ronald Reagan offered Bush the vice presidential spot on the ticket. George knew he wasn't the first choice. And he knew that Reagan had some doubts about him. But once he was chosen, all the fighting between them stopped. Reagan saw Bush and himself as a partnership. They would run and serve together, as a team. When they first met, Reagan said: "Let's get one thing clear, George. You're on the ticket with me because you're different from me. If I wanted a Reagan clone, I would have picked one."

The Reagan-Bush ticket won a smashing victory. The two men took the oath of office on January 21, 1981. The Vice President was usually something of an outsider in the White House. President Reagan changed that. He went out of his way to bring Bush inside the White House circle. Their trust and friendship grew every day.

On March 30—just two months after he took office—President Reagan was shot by John Hinckley, Jr., in Washington, D.C. At that moment Bush was in the air over Texas, en route to Austin, the state capital. A Secret Service agent rushed up to him and said an attempt had been made on the President's life. The President was all right, he said, but "two agents and Jim Brady were hit." Jim Brady was Reagan's press secretary. At first Bush was going to continue to Austin to make a speech. But moments later a call came from Alexander Haig, Secretary of State: "There's been an incident. The feeling is you ought to return to Washington as soon as possible."

Haig said a coded message would follow. The cabin phone buzzed again. It was Donald Regan, Secretary of the Treasury. He told Bush to forget the Austin speech and fly back to Washington immediately. The Secret Service agent's earlier report only told part of the story. The President had been shot and rushed into emergency surgery. Bush ordered the plane to Washington.

When he arrived in the capital, some government officials rushed up to him. They thought it would reassure the country if Bush was seen on television taking control. He would step out of a helicopter on the White House south lawn. Bush thought it was wrong to do that. He said, "Only the President lands on the south lawn." It was Bush's rule for being a good Vice President. The country could have only one President at a time—and the Vice

President shouldn't act like the President.

Reagan was reported to be out of danger, but needed time to recover before going back to work. So when Bush took over the President's duties, he clearly understood his role as Vice President:

"It never occurred to me—even for a fleeting moment—that I was anything more than a stand-in. But this brings it home."

Bush was praised for the way he took control in Reagan's absence. He operated from his own office in the White House. He conducted Cabinet meetings from his own chair—leaving Reagan's chair empty. He did what was necessary, and never more than that. The President recovered quickly, and Bush returned to his vice presidential duties.

Bush was aware that he had become Vice President because of Reagan's popularity, and he owed him loyalty and support. "He is the most loyal team member anyone could want," said the President. Larry Speakes, a former White House press secretary, said, "Bush was the perfect team player, the perfect 'yes' man."

Like most politicians Bush had his supporters—people who liked him and thought he did a good job as Vice President. And Bush had his critics. "Nobody ever went to him for help," said Elliott Abrams, the Assistant Secretary of State. "I can't ever remember him speaking up at meetings." Another White House aide said, "I was at hundreds of meetings with Bush, and I had no idea what he really thought."

Friends said that in private he had strong opinions, and he could be very stubborn. A former Bush aide said, "I have no doubts about George Bush's toughness. Outside he's all New England gentleman. But when he closes the door, he's all Texas-tough." Some officials in the administration said that Bush was unusually well-informed, fair, and could get to the heart of *any* problem.

In 1984, Reagan and Bush ran for re-election. During that campaign, Bush was criticized by political observers. They said he should have been more honest with the public when he disagreed with President Reagan. Bush felt that a Vice President could have a different opinion from the

President. He could discuss it with the President in private. He could try to change the President's mind. But once the President made his decision, the matter was settled.

There were other bad moments in the campaign. A televised debate took place between Bush and Geraldine Ferraro, the Democratic candidate for Vice President, and the first woman to run for that office. During the debate, Bush treated Ferraro, a smart woman, like a political amateur. She was having trouble making a point and Bush broke in, "Let me help . . . " Ferraro met his remark with anger. "I resent your patronizing attitude, Vice President Bush." He was declared the winner of the debate by the press and television reporters. Yet overnight Ferraro rose in the polls, while Bush dropped.

When making a campaign speech, Bush discussed an Israeli invasion of Lebanon where two hundred and fifty American Marines were sent to keep the peace and were killed in an Arab terrorist explosion. He claimed that Walter Mondale, the

Democratic presidential candidate, and Geraldine Ferraro had said those Marines had "died in shame." This was a grave error, as neither Democratic candidate had said that, and the party reacted with outrage.

It was days before Bush apologized for this incident. Instead, with TV cameras rolling, he searched dictionaries for different meanings of *shame* to prove his point. Afraid that Bush's marred image would look more and more foolish, the Reagan staff cut short his public appearances for a time.

The campaign did have its ups and downs, but on election day in 1984 the Reagan-Bush ticket was reelected, winning forty-nine of the fifty states—a landslide.

Along the Campaign Trail

During his second term as Vice President, Bush was talked up as the leading Republican candidate for President in 1988. He was sure he would make a good President. Even a top Democrat saw his confidence. Tip O'Neill, then Speaker of the House of Representatives, said:

"All you have to do is walk down the street with George, and you know he thinks he can be President."

On the surface he had all the qualities that voters liked. He was a very attractive man, physically and personally. He was friendly, and easy with all classes of people. He made friends wherever he went— and was almost impossible to dislike.

But there were doubts about his fitness for the role of President.

Pat Buchanan, the conservative columnist, worked at the White House for a time. He said, "Bush is a real sweetheart of a human being. Everybody at the White House respects him as a person. But they do not see him as a strong political leader. There are a lot of question marks about him."

At the start of the 1988 campaign the polls said voters doubted if he was truly serious, and if he could think for himself. People weren't sure that he had enough personal strength, or whether he could make decisions on his own.

Almost all of Bush's work as Vice President was hidden. There were a few exceptions. He led various government groups that did excellent work. They fought drugs and terrorism. Bush helped to get rid of many useless government rules. In 1985— despite objections by the State Department and the Pentagon—he airlifted eight hundred Ethiopian Jews to Israel. He saved them from starvation. He got the El Salvador military to stop its death squads. And he had thirty billion dollars in tax breaks restored to the big oil companies. In his two terms as Vice President Bush flew over a million miles and was out of the country a hundred and sixty days visiting seventy-four foreign countries. But his critics said his main function seemed to be attending the funerals of foreign leaders.

In 1988 Bush ran a poor third in the first nominating election in Iowa. He needed a win in New Hampshire or he might quickly be out of the race for President. He came from behind and won a big victory. Then, on a day called Super Tuesday, he won sixteen of the seventeen primaries in the South. Even before the Republican convention in New Orleans, Bush had won enough support to become the party's candidate. It would become official at the convention. After Super Tuesday, Bush said, "I'm now convinced I will be the President of the United States." But even though Bush was a conservative, there were many conservative newspaper columnists and politicians against him. Some said his campaign speeches sounded too much like the Democrats. Others called his campaign "hot air" and "baloney," and said he couldn't be elected.

During the primaries, Bush told Reagan

supporters that he would protect the Reagan programs. They could trust him. But Bush had a problem. Should he run on the Reagan record—or move away from it if it meant votes? If he strayed too far from the Reagan record, it would drive away conservative voters. But he had to show people he had his own ideas.

One Bush adviser said: "After Ronald Reagan, people may be looking for another John Wayne. Well, George Bush isn't John Wayne. He's more like a western sheriff who doesn't want to fight. He'd rather talk things out. But if it's necessary to fight—he'll fight—and he'll whip you."

George Bush had to make people believe he had that kind of courage. He had to learn not to be so careful. He had to be his own man—to say what he was for and against. That wouldn't be easy. Bush was a careful, practical, moderate man. He had to know how far he could move away from Reagan and not be charged with disloyalty. It seemed he would be in trouble if he did, and in trouble if he didn't. By May, when his nomination was assured, he began to move away in small ways. He said he would be "more concerned with education and the environment" . . . "more aggressive in attacking" the unbalanced budget . . . "give more support to social programs."

Unlike Reagan, Bush didn't have any set ideas or political philosophy:

"I am a practical man," he said. "I like what's real. I like what works. I don't want to lead a crusade. But a President can set a tone, give moral leadership."

Bush set out to bring his vision of America to the public: "We face some pretty difficult challenges in the years ahead. But the word *challenge* is just another word for opportunity. If we seize these opportunities, we can lead America into a new era of peace and prosperity. We live in the freest, fairest, the most generous nation on earth. Most people have faith in America—and I'll always defend this great land. I plan to help lead it. I want to spread the light of freedom. The idea of America is just as good today as it was two hundred years ago."

Bush campaigned hard and long before the Republican convention. In a speech in

New York City he said it was time to get tough with drug peddlers and people who murdered police officers. Bush said he favored the death penalty for people who killed police officers. Then he challenged his Democratic opponents to say there should be a war on drugs, conducted like a real war, and not to let killers back on the streets. He demanded to know what the Democrats were doing about the drug problem.

"Many of them criticize. But how many of them have been for tougher jail sentences for those who poison our kids? How many of them support our police?"

Bush said that the Coast Guard needed to hire more staff to stop drug smugglers. The Vice President said he'd find new ways to stop countries from producing drugs, and he wanted an international drug force under the United Nations. Bush spoke out against racism and called it "a great sadness." He said, "We are on the journey to a new century. We must finally leave behind the tired old baggage of hate and bigotry."

He promised to reach out to all minorities. He would listen to their complaints and do something if he were President. To win in 1988, Bush needed the support of many minority groups. And they often voted for the Democratic candidate.

In July of 1988, Michael S. Dukakis, the governor of Massachusetts, became the Democratic candidate for President. Right after the convention, Dukakis was leading Bush in the polls. Bush received advice from many Republicans. Some said he had to keep running on Reagan's record. Others said he had to be his own man. Bush had understood his problem as far back as 1986. He spoke at a Conservative party dinner in New York:

"Some people say I don't have much of a political future if I don't put distance between myself and the President. Well, even if it costs me my political career, I won't do that. . . . Maybe it's the old Navy pilot in me—but you don't cut and run on your friends."

Meanwhile, Barbara Bush was also out

campaigning. She took along a slide show—scenes from the life of George and Barbara Bush:

George at the Wall of the Second Temple in Jerusalem . . . at the Berlin Wall . . . the Great Wall of China . . . George with many world leaders . . . George jogging . . . George playing tennis . . . scenes of the Bushes at Walker's Point in Maine . . . the family sailing . . . grandchildren running around the Bush bed . . .

Mrs. Bush hoped to show "the warmth of George and the love of his family, how active he is. I wanted people to know his wife who loves him and has enormous respect for him."

She talked about the pain of the public spotlight. She heard unkind talk about herself—her makeup, her gray hair, and stout figure. Some joked that she looked like Bush's mother. "I tell you the truth, it hurts," Barbara said. Once, a television interviewer said to her, "Your husband is a man of the 1980s. You're a woman of the 1940s. What do you say to that?" Mrs. Bush said she almost burst into tears.

Barbara said she didn't regret dropping

out of college to get married and didn't regret not having a career. Being a wife and raising five children was career enough. She said the Bushes weren't "out of touch" with other Americans because their families were wealthy.

"It would be outrageous if I said we were ever hungry. But in those early days in Texas, we weren't kings and queens."

She hated hearing that Bush was not his own man, that he didn't have a strong personality. " . . . I think he has charisma . . . I want him to win because I think he's the best man for the job."

The Final Lap

The Republican convention opened in New Orleans, Louisiana, on August 15, 1988. George Bush would soon be the official Republican candidate for President. Bush needed a good start in his campaign, and there was only one way to get it: he had to give a strong, inspiring speech at the convention. He had to show voters that he was his own man. He had to prove that he had his own ideas about the issues of the election.

Bush had never been known as a good speaker. His manner was stiff, his voice a kind of high-pitched whine. There was danger that if his speech went poorly, his campaign would fall flat before it started. But that night, the most important of his political life, George Bush gave his best speech ever. His voice was strong and dramatic, in command.

He began by paying respect to President

Ronald Reagan. But he quickly showed that he wasn't going to depend on the public's love for the President. He showed that now *he* was the man in charge of the party's future.

"Now you see me for what I am," he said on national television to the convention delegates—"the Republican candidate for the President of the United States."

For the first time George Bush gave a glimpse of the private man beneath the public mask. He admitted to certain faults and turned them into something positive.

"I may not be the most eloquent. I may sometimes be a little awkward," Bush said. "But there is nothing self-conscious in my love of country. I am a quiet man—but I hear the quiet people others don't. The quiet people who raise the family, pay the taxes, meet the mortgage. I hear them, and their concerns are mine."

He spoke about family and freedom and the American future. He promised to create thirty million new jobs if he were elected President. With great skill he presented himself as the man to carry on Reagan's programs. But he also made people believe he was now his own man. He was ready, he said, to sit behind the big desk in the President's Oval Office.

"This election, what it all comes down to, after all the shouting and cheers—is the man at the desk. And who should sit at that desk? My friends—I am that man!"

Two days before his speech Bush made a decision that would hurt the early stages of his campaign. He had been silent about his choice for Vice President. He had smart political advisers, but he said, "I want to do this one myself." He then announced his running mate. It was Indiana Senator Dan Quayle. Quayle, only forty-one years old, was a boyishly good-looking conservative who was not well known outside his own state.

Many people disliked Bush's choice for Vice President. Quayle was the first of his generation—the generation that had come of age during the Vietnam War—to run for national office. His service during the Vietnam War was questioned. Instead of going to Vietnam to fight, Quayle had served at home in the National Guard. Many people thought that Americans should not be sent to fight in Vietnam. But Quayle believed it was right for Americans to do so. There was no shame enlisting in the National Guard. Many young men did. But Quayle, in his public career, had always been pro-military. So some people criticized him for not practicing what he preached. Some also thought he had used his wealthy family's connections to get into the National Guard to avoid fighting in Vietnam.

Quayle made matters worse in his first press conference and speeches. Reporters asked him about the Vietnam question. Sometimes he gave one answer and sometimes another. He seemed very nervous.

Bush refused to drop Quayle. He said he had no doubts about his running mate:

"Not me, not me. I remain cool in all these crises because I've been there. . . . I have my confidence in the new generation and in Dan Quayle. And wait until you see this guy on job training and national defense. You'll be as proud of him as I am."

Bush began his campaign with a quick swing through Texas, California, Oregon, Missouri, and Tennessee. But he was no longer the gentlemanly, often hesitant Vice President the public had seen. He came out fighting!

Bush said that Dukakis was wrong for vetoing a Massachusetts bill that required the Pledge of Allegiance to be recited daily in the public schools. Michael Dukakis said he vetoed the bill because it was unconstitutional. But he was *for* a voluntary pledge to the flag in the classrooms.

"What is it about the Pledge of Allegiance that upsets him so much? It's very hard for me to imagine that the Founding Fathers would have objected to teachers leading students in the Pledge of Allegiance to the United States."

Dukakis quickly answered: "The American people aren't interested in a debate over which one of us loves his country most. We all love our country. There should be no debate on that."

Bush talked about all the years of a Republican economy that was stable and growing. Many people were better off than they had been under Jimmy Carter, the most recent Democratic President. Under President Reagan Americans had had peace and prosperity. Bush kept telling the voters that it was the Republicans who had provided the good times. He knew the public believed in a trusted American saying: "If it ain't broke, don't fix it." In other words, don't vote for the unknown— Dukakis.

Michael Dukakis wanted Bush to debate him on the issues. He wanted three or four debates. Bush agreed to only two. Bush knew Dukakis was a fine debater. The Massachusetts governor had hosted a television debating program called *The Advocates*. "I have respect for him as a debater," Bush said. "Mr. Dukakis is far better than I am." He didn't seem to want to go one on one against Dukakis. But the two debate dates were set. The first one took place on September 25, 1988. At last the voters could see both men together—and measure one against the other. The second one took place on October 13th.

The campaign was hard-fought all the way. The two candidates began to argue about the big issues instead of attacking each other so much. Each candidate tried to show the voters that he could lead the country in tackling its real needs in a tough world. Just before Election Day—November 8, 1988—Bush returned to Houston, Texas, and Dukakis to Brookline, Massachusetts, to vote.

It was time for the public to make a decision. The winner would direct the course of American life, power, and prosperity almost into the next century. The polls showed George Bush was way ahead.

As he awaited the election results, George Bush, as always, seemed confident. He had been in public life for twenty-five years. Now the Presidency—the biggest chal-lenge of all—was almost in his grasp—but he must have been bothered by some questions.

Had his harsh style of campaigning turned off many voters?

Had he—finally—created a strong public image and made people feel confident in him?

Had his choice of Dan Quayle hurt him?

Bush was soon to find out. Results poured in from state after state, and at last the people's choice became clear. George Bush won the election! He became the forty-first President of the United States.

Late that night, Bush stood with his family before a crowd of cheering supporters in Houston. He was very tired, but he was happy. "The people have spoken," he said. And they had spoken for *him*. Now George Bush was ready to face the challenges yet to come.

Glossary

bill—A written proposal for a law. If Congress and the President approve a *bill*, it becomes a law.

campaign—A plan for winning an election. A person *campaigns* by giving speeches, by asking people to vote for him or her, by debating opponents, by displaying banners and posters, and by advertising on TV.

candidate—A person who wants to be voted into office. George Bush and Michael Dukakis were *candidates* for the office of President of the United States.

civil rights—Rights belonging to every member of society, such as the right to go to school, to live where you want to, or to get a job you are qualified for. In the 1960s black people worked to gain their *civil rights*.

Congress—A nation's lawmaking body, made up of representatives from all parts of the country. The U.S. *Congress* has two parts: the House of Representatives and the Senate.

conservative—A person (or belief) who likes things the way they are, is cautious about change, wants to take things step by step. *Conservatives* often believe that the government should play as small a role as possible in people's lives.

Constitution—A set of rules for running the country. It is the President's job to make sure people live by the *Constitution*.

delegate—A representative to the Republican or Democratic National Convention. Party members in each state choose their state's *delegates*. At the conventions the delegates nominate and vote for their party's candidate.

Democrat—A member of one of the two major political parties in the U.S. *Democrats* are usually considered more liberal than Republicans.

economy—The management of a country's money and resources. When the *economy* is good, many people have jobs and are able to spend money on the goods and services they need.

liberal—A person (or belief) who likes change, reform, progress. *Liberals* often believe that the government should play a large part in people's lives.

nominate—To choose or name a person to run for political office. The Republican party *nominated* George Bush to run for President.

nominee—A person who has been chosen to run for political office. George Bush was the Republican *nominee* for President.

platform—A political party's feelings about certain issues, such as crime, health care, and taxes. The party's *platform* is decided on at the convention.

policy—A guideline used by a government or political party to help make decisions. The way a government behaves toward other countries is its foreign *policy*.

political convention—A meeting of the delegates from a political party. At the *convention* the delegates (1) choose candidates to run for President and Vice President, and (2) decide how the party will stand on the issues of the election.

poll—1. The place where people vote. 2. A group of questions asked of many people and then tallied and reported. In a recent *poll* many Americans said that drugs was the number one problem in the U.S.

primary—A state election in which members of each political party choose a candidate to run for office. To become the Republican candidate, George Bush had to win more *primaries* than anyone else.

prosperity—The ability to live comfortably, to be well-off. *Prosperous* people are not the richest people, but they have everything they need as well as some luxuries.

record—The history of a candidate's actions; what he or she has voted for and against. A candidate's *record* shows what is really important to him or her.

representative—A member of a lawmaking group, such as the House of Representatives in Congress. A class might select a *representative* to attend a student council meeting.

Republican—A member of one of the two major political parties in the U.S. *Republicans* are usually thought to be more conservative than Democrats.

Senate—1. A lawmaking group; part of Congress. 2. The place where lawmakers meet. The U.S. *Senate* has one hundred members, two Senators from each of the fifty states.

Senator—A lawmaker who may work in the U.S. Senate or a state senate. Each state elects two *senators* to serve in the U.S. Congress.

unconstitutional—Not in keeping with the laws of the Constitution. To force people to say the Pledge of Allegiance when it is against their beliefs is unconstitutional.

veto—The right of a President or other leader to say "no." When the President doesn't want to sign a new law, he *vetoes* it.